A Man of Letters

A comedy on the edge of a building

Tim Firth

Samuel French—London
New York - Toronto - Hollywood

A MAN OF LETTERS

First performed at the Stephen Joseph Theatre in the Round Studio, Scarborough, 1991.

Frank   Jeffrey Chiswick

Alan   Gary Whitaker

Directed by Connal Orton
Designed by Juliet Nichols

The action takes place on a ledge halfway up a business unit.

Time—the present

For Richard, Rosemary and May.
And all the Franks.

AUTHOR'S NOTE

A word about letters.

The letters are collectively the third character in this two-hander. Part of the challenge is meeting the rather unusual stage requirements of several, large, bright red three-dimensional letters, strong enough in some cases to sit and stand on. Keeping them box-shaped and angular seems to be the key. In the Scarborough production they were built from wood, and by bevelling some of the right-angled edges there was no need for any curves at all. The round letters (**a**, **e** and **o**) were effectively adapted squares, which then meant the **o**, for example, was easily strong enough to sit on. The tallest letter, the capital **F**, was made stable by weighting the bottom, and because the **r** and **n** were all right angles, fitting them together provided a very striking capital **S**.

One way of making them light up at the end is to fake the electric cable on stage, and cover or outline the letters in a particular paint or cord (the kind used by D. J.s) which reacts to ultra violet light. Some u.v. tubes hidden behind the front ledge can then be cued to come on at the moment of black-out, giving a very effective "flickering on" effect. The letter **o** has to be made to look like the others, but should not react to the u.v. light, so that, in the final tableau, it doesn't light up.

Alternatively, you can always contact the Stephen Joseph Theatre in Scarborough about the possibility of hiring the original production letters.

A MAN OF LETTERS

*We are on an empty ledge perched high on the side of a business unit in
the north of England*

*Between the front lip of the ledge and the back wall there is enough room
to move freely about, but not exactly acres of space. Set into that back
wall and giving out on to the ledge is a large sliding window. Through
it we can see part of a spartan office with a filing cabinet and the
statutory dying plant, which committed suicide some months ago and
has turned brown*

UL *is a wall-mounted electricity junction box. Off the front there is a drop
of about sixty feet and the wind blows up the sound of traffic noise over
the initial music. This insect-like background hum is noticeable when-
ever there is a pause on stage*

*The Lights come up. The music fades as voices emerge from off stage.
The window is shut so they are initially muffled. Frank and Alan are
struggling — but we can't see what with. Frank has the tone of an
impatient father force-feeding his son with a lifetime of knowledge*

Frank (*off*) Steady. Steady. Don't push. Look, you're pushing.

> *Frank suddenly rockets with some force into the filing cabinet, at the
> front of a long red object. He is a well-worn fifty-four. He is wearing
> a donkey jacket and carefully-ironed blue overalls with a meticulously
> presented shirt and tie underneath. He carries a leather toolkit over
> his shoulder*

I'm at the filing cabinet, aren't I? I'm at the filing cabinet. (*He
gestures*) Swing it round. Back ... back off.

Still out of vision, Alan turns the object around. Frank swivels his back to the cabinet

Now, is it going to go through like that? Is it going to go through that way? No, it's not, Alan.

They move the object on its end

That's better. Right. (*He produces a huge ring of keys and unlocks the window*) The people who triumph in life are the ones that think one step ahead, Alan. Remember that. (*He slides it open and breathes in the fresh wind*) It's like snooker. Any Tom, Dick, or Harry can knock the red in. Steve Davis sets himself up for the black afterwards. Hitch her up. Steady. (*He starts to back through the window, carrying a huge red box structure, with two prongs*) Now watch me, all right. I ease myself through, OK? I ease through and I know, Alan, that there's a sixty foot drop off the ledge there. I know that, 'cos I've checked, OK? So I think, just in case there's a cross-wind, I'll stay close to the building, right? Now I've worked that out between the vending machine and here, OK? That's what you have to learn. Lower ... and release.

*They deposit a large red capital **F** on the floor, prongs upwards to the sky. Frank straightens up and looks out, wiping his forehead. That hurt*

Alan stands, dully. He is a slightly gauche, awkward eighteen, wearing trainers, scruffy jeans and a hooded top with the hood up

Good. And so you see, she's pristine. Not a scratch. And that's important. Lesson one. It has to mean as much to you as it does to Mister Forshaw that his name's up here right. Pride. Lesson one.

Pause. Alan stands, dully, wincing out towards the horizon, with a slightly gormless expression on his face. Frank turns to look out

But that's your reward. No-one else gets to see that view. Apart from them in that office, but they're looking at it through glass. This is pure.

Just you, the air and the A12 bypass. And that's, looking south, that's the Pennines. On a clear day you can see Preston's Folly up there, did you know that? Lord Preston, seventeen eighty-two, built this arch on the top of the crag for no reason. Beautiful great arch, just like as his … legacy for all time.

Pause. His face falls slightly

And now it's got "Lorraine-heart-Gary" carved all over it. I tell you she gets about, that girl. Everything round us has got bloody "Lorraine" carved in it somewhere. I think she must be paid by the council. She couldn't do it part time. It's like the Forth Bridge. Once she's finished going round the estate, the Tippex'll be wearing off the first phone box, so she starts again. I can't give people directions round my estate anymore. It's "turn right into Lorraine Crescent, follow it round till you get to Fascist Police Scum and it's the third Lorraine on the left." (*He carries on staring out*) Is it like that round you?

Alan just stares out, dully. He winces

I said, is it like that round you?(*Pause*) I'm not going too fast for you, Alan, am I? (*Pause. He turns round*) Are there any questions you want to ask?

Alan sees Frank looking at him. So he pulls down his hood and removes the personal stereo headphones which he has been wearing throughout all this

Alan Eh?

Frank looks at him, stricken, his mouth searching for words. We feel a whole grand canyon open up between them

Frank I'm not recapping, Alan. I'm not going back over this. I'm not — you can't send off for worksheets at the end of the programme. This is it. There's kids queueing up down there, give their right arm to be doing employment training up here, and you're stood there listening to George-flaming-Rod Stewart. Get it off. Give it here.

Alan dully removes the stereo and gives it to Frank

Go and get that next one. Go on.

Alan retreats clumsily through the back window

Frank watches him go. He shakes his head gently. He sits

And the Lord did sow some seeds upon the barren ground.

He looks at the Walkman. He presses the button. It squawks furiously through the headphones. Frank stops it. He takes the tape out. He pauses

The defector, Ivan Bulgovsky, removed the tape from the machine. He turned it round in his old wizened fingers, like a toy. He tapped it on one of his old, wizened fingers. (*He does so*) The very finger which dialled the number which got him into all this. He stood up. (*He stands*) He huddled his coat round him, a huge mammoth of a coat, like an old bear carcass, only from Burton's. He laughed to himself. Ah ha. That was quite funny. Or maybe it wasn't. He didn't know anymore. (*He huddles*) The Leningrad wind had bitter teeth. He remembered someone saying there were no mountains between here and Stowmarket in East Anglia. But, oh, East Anglia seemed far away now. He closed his eyes and he were back in Cambridge, stretched out on the banks of the river, with a bottle of champagne in one hand and a copy of Wittgenstein, signed by the author, in the other. And there, drifting downstream towards him was Anatevka, her auburn hair catching the yellow light off King's College Chapel. The plop of her punt pole plopping in the water filled the air. For a moment, neither of them spoke. The afternoon, the architecture said it all. Then, softly, with the warmth of twenty summers, Anatevka looked up, her voice full of mystery and brooding enchantment.

Alan (*off; shouting*) D'you want a Twix, Frank?

Frank is wounded

Frank Forget the Twix! Forget the flamin' Twix. The government didn't set this scheme up for you to eat Twixes.

Silence. Frank looks at the tape. He recomposes himself

> How was he to know she were part Russian? How was he to know
> where that one kiss would lead? One kiss. One affair. One one-way
> ticket to Leningrad.

A loud glass-smash is heard off

> Oh for God's sake. *Alan. (He goes back to peer through the windows)*
> These are delicate things. They don't bounce. Here.

They both hoick through a large red lower case letter **a**

> Let's get it out of harm's way. There. Now what is it? What've you
> broken?

Alan Snowstorm.

Pause

Frank *(slowly)* What language are you hearing me in? God, sometimes
I think I need an English-into-Alan phrasebook. *(He points at his lips)*
Watch. What — did — you …?

Alan Snowstorm. It was a paperweight with a snowstorm in it.

Frank *(sinking in)* Tracey's? Off that desk there?

Alan Greetings from Reykjavik.

Frank Oh well that's only Tracey's paperweight you've gone and
broken. Her boyfriend bought her that. He's an agricultural sales rep.
(Slight pause. He sighs, pointedly) I'll have to write a note now. *(He
retreats to lean his paper on a letter)* We can't have hamfisted people
in this job. You *look* where you're going. Especially on *this* job. These
are my offices, all right? These are the people I have to work with
everyday, all right?

Alan Mmm.

*While Frank writes, Alan peers over the edge at the drop. He has a
laddish go at throwing spit on passers-by*

Frank (*scribbling*) "Dear Tracey. It's your old mate Frank from the works department. Brackets head close brackets. A thousand apologies for broken paperweight. We all have a cross to bear in life. Mine is called Alan.

Frank looks at Alan, who immediately buckles upright

He will be paying. Love Frank." Right. Go and put that on her desk.
Alan Which one?
Frank (*after a pause*) The — one — with — the — snow — on — it.

Alan goes back into the office

Frank turns. He sees the letter **a** *which has been deposited. He puts one hand on his head*

Alan. *Alan.*

Alan reappears at the window

How d'you spell Forshaw?

Alan looks at him, suspiciously

Come on. It's not quantum physics. Forshaw. The name. How d'you spell it?
Alan (*treading on coals*) F ... o ...
Frank Right. Let's just stop there. Let's see where we're going wrong so far, OK?
Alan The o's at the back.
Frank F-o-r-s-h-a-w.
Alan (*louder*) The o's at the back.

Frank composes himself

Frank There are two kinds of people in life, Alan. The kind who get things in order in the depot, and the kind who end up on top of a business unit juggling armfuls of letters and killing someone with a six foot h. Now what d'you want to be, eh?

Pause. Alan shrugs. Frank mimes Alan's shrug

And what's that? That's a gesture of dynamism, is it?

Huge pause. Alan shrugs again

(*Pointing*) No-one who shrugged ever got anywhere in life. Presidents of the United States, Paul McCartney — "Shall we go and write a song, Paul?" (*He shrugs*) "I'm not faffed." You don't get anywhere. People who shrug end up ... under the rug. (*He nods*) Now that isn't a saying, but it could be. In fact, it should be, because they achieve nothing. There's a room, Alan, in hell reserved for shruggers and someone asked if they wanted a cup of tea three hundred years ago and they've been shrugging ever since. (*He moves the* **a**)

Alan Is it tea then, now?

Frank looks up

Frank Tea?
Alan You said tea.

Frank stares in disbelief

Frank Come here.

He sits Alan down on the prostrate letter **F**

I'm going to tell you something in confidence. Mister Forshaw who's bought this place over, I talked to him last week, in confidence. Now we don't know this, all right, but all this is going to expand. And when it does, the people who'll get first in the job queue aren't the ones standing at the back wondering when the tea break's coming. You understand what I'm saying?

Alan (*dully*) Yeh.

Frank And he told me in confidence that as long as there was a lettering plant here I'd be head of works, and he did that because he knows I don't spend my time looking forward to tea breaks.

Alan (*sighing*) Yeh.

Frank And he, (*kicking the* **F**) isn't getting his name on the front of this building because he kept looking forward to tea breaks. There are bigger things than tea breaks in life, Alan. Much bigger things. D'you understand what I'm saying?

Alan Yeh. (*He nods. Pause. He looks down*) Lunch.

Frank (*after a slight pause*) *Not lunch.* Not anything to do with food. *Ambition.* Achievement. He will have known since he was eighteen, sevent —— *seven* that he wanted his name up on buildings. He'll've had that here. (*Hand to his stomach*) Same with me, I knew. (*After a slight pause; accusingly*) What did you want to do when you were seven?

Alan Don't know.

Frank Precisely. And so here you are ten years later shrugging and looking forward to tea breaks.

Alan No-one knows when they're seven.

Frank What?

Alan What they want to be.

Frank You're arguing?

Alan I wanted to be in *Grange Hill*.

Frank I'm talking realistically. All right, Mr Forshaw didn't write in his diary "When I grow up I want to be the owner of a plastic commercial lettering service in Leeds", but he knew he wanted to succeed, that's what I'm saying. In here. (*His hand to his stomach*)

Alan Oh.

Frank Right? Lesson learnt?

Alan (*slightly hangdog*) Yeh.

Frank Now go and get the next one.

Alan gets up to go, dully. Frank softens a moment. He decides to play the godfather

   Hey, and Alan? (*He winks matily and chucks him a coin*) Have a cup of tea on me, eh?

Frank smiles, paternally. Alan looks at the coin

Alan There i'n't any.
Frank What?
Alan There i'n't any.
Frank There's no tea? You let me go through all that and there's no tea anyway?
Alan S'what I was going to tell you.
Frank There's a vending machine.
Alan It's gone.
Frank It were there five minutes ago.
Alan It's gone.
Frank What, it waited till we went past, then made a break for it?
Alan (*shrugging*) Dunno.
Frank (*pointing*) Don't shrug. Go down to the third floor machine. By Brian's office. That's the design department machine, but if there's any trouble, tell them Frank, head of works, sent you.
Alan You want tea, then?
Frank (*after a pause*) I do now. I'm thirsty now. But it's not a tea break. I want the next modules up here. And a biscuit.

Alan takes the money and trudges off. He trudges back

Alan What if that one's gone as well?
Frank It won't have gone. They're not planning a coup. Go on.

Alan trudges off

Frank has a coin. He looks out at the view, then he spins the coin

He spun a coin. (*He spins it again, catches it and looks at it*) Heads. That were three hundred and seven heads, three hundred and seven tails. Bulgovsky suddenly realized how long he'd been waiting on the bridge. Yet his mathematical Cambridge mind couldn't let him leave without finding which way the last throw would go. He flicked the rouble high into the Leningrad night. (*He mimes it and watches it go up and up …*) It hung for a second, a few feet nearer to God before plummeting down towards the dark, troubled earth. A hand caught it. (*After a pause*) But it was not Bulgovsky's. (*He pauses. He smiles*) End paragraph. Three asterisks. Blank page. Chapter Two.

He pauses. Somewhere in his thoughts, Frank is lost; somewhere he is on a Leningrad Bridge. Then his eyes dull a little. His smile decreases one notch. He sits on the **F** *in a staged pose, as if for a photograph*

(*Talking through his teeth*) Frank Tollit began writing in nineteen sixty-three. (*He pulls a thoughtful pose*) His early influences were John le Carré, Frederick Forsyth and Len Deighton. (*He stages a moody, sullen pose*) During his early years as a boy he was a close compatriot of Tony Bell, who later became Anthony Belgravia. (*He lounges back on the prongs of the* **F**) He lives on the Roecastle Council Estate with his wife, the actress and model Jane Seymour.

Pause

They have two children. Jeremy, nineteen, who is at Cambridge University and also plays for Spurs, and Christina, seventeen, who is at finishing school in Switzerland.

There is a huge glass-smash off. Frank starts up

Right. That's it. *Out here.*
Alan (*off, protesting*) I'm carrying an o.
Frank Out here. That's the last time you go off unsupervised. Come on.
Alan (*off*) I've got tea and an o.
Frank Other people manage, Alan.

Alan emerges

Alan Not tea *and* an o.
Frank Waitresses at the *Berni Inn* carry seven plates at once. Pass it here.

A large red lower case **o** *is hoicked through the window with tea and biscuits balanced on the top*

What did you break? What did you break?

Alan The snowstorm.
Frank Again?
Alan It fell into the bin.
Frank It jumped for safety more like. Come here. Here.

Frank steers Alan to the edge of the ledge, Alan a little wary that Frank might be chucking him off

Alan. That is a sixty-foot drop. This is a ledge. There is very little difference between the two.

Alan peers over

And I'm telling you. This is Wembley Stadium compared to what you normally get. Which is why hamfisted, clumsy letterers find it very difficult to get partners.
Alan I don't *like* it. I don't *like* being clumsy.

There is an odd pause. Frank feels slightly chastened

Frank Yes, well. (*He doesn't quite know what to say*)

Alan, wounded, gives him the tea and then sits on the **F**

Any trouble?

Alan shakes his head. Frank opens his tea and sits on the **O**

Did you see anyone?

Alan shakes his head. Frank finds the plastic-wrapped pair of digestives

What's this?
Alan Digestives. 'S all they had.

Frank views the spartan biscuit with considerable disappointment. He unwraps it. He looks at it. He nibbles it. Alan produces a Twix. He unwraps it and bites. Frank stops dead and stares at him

Frank Excuse me.

Alan stops dead, his mouth full. Frank looks at his digestives, then at Alan's Twix. Alan looks at his Twix, his mouth full, not chewing

How come the Twix fairy didn't stop at my house?

Alan You said biscuit.

Frank Twix is a biscuit. "Smooth milk chocolate, chewy caramel on a crunchy biscuit base". Biscuit.

Alan It's a sweet. Biscuits don't have chocolate.

Frank Oh like, so what, chocolate digestives, that's not a biscuit?

Alan Except chocolate biscuits.

Frank Chocolate Hobnobs, they're not biscuits, they're ... they're ... they're caravans?

Alan *Except chocolate biscuits.*

Frank No, you carry on. You carry on with your Twix. I'll just tuck into my double-whipped cream caramel flake flaming plain digestives. (*He disdainfully takes a mouthful*)

Alan (*quietly*) You said digestives.

Frank I mean, it's a little thing, it's just ... (*The words reach him*) I didn't say digestives. I said biscuit.

Alan Biscuit, I mean.

Frank I happen to know I never actually said the word "digestive", because I use the word "McVities" or "Homewheat".

Alan All right, "biscuit", not "digestive".

Frank I mean, it's just a little thing, but we do have sometimes to remember, in life, who is the YTS trainee ——

Alan (*quietly*) It's not YTS.

Frank —— and who is the head of works, the overall head of works, in this company. Giving out twenty-five years worth of experience, all neatly packaged up ...

Alan D'you want a Twix?

Frank All free. And little things like who gets Twixes or digestives, it doesn't matter to *me* ...

Alan Do you want a Twix?

Frank I don't mind. But there are other people in this company who ——

Alan (*loudly*) Look, have a flaming Twix.

He produces a fistful of Twixes out his jacket. Frank is immediately silenced

   Go on, have four.
Frank (*quietly*) Where d'you get them all from?
Alan The machine. They were giving 'em away.

Frank looks at the Twix and then at Alan

Frank And here's me putting twenty-two p in every time and there's a button that gives them away. *Where d'you get them from?*
Alan Blokes were giving them out.
Frank People don't give away Twixes, Alan. It doesn't happen. The day they start giving away Twixes the ravens'll leave the Tower of London.
Alan It's true.
Frank The first signs of the apocalypse. The mountains sink, the seas boil and folk start handing out Twixes.
Alan The blokes did it who were taking the machine away.

Pause

Frank What, permanently?
Alan I don't know, do I? I don't work here.

Frank registers this as odd. He eats his biscuit

Frank Must be a problem with them all.

Pause

Alan D'you always do that?
Frank What?
Alan You always do that: taking a sentence then going on and on about it.
Frank What's that supposed to mean?
Alan The ravens. Then all that after it. About Twixes and the seas boiling.

Frank (*studiedly*) The ravens re the Twix is called a metaphor. Going "on and on about it" is called an extended metaphor.

Alan D'you know all about that?

Frank Course I know all about that. I'm a writer. I have to. It's like a gardener not knowing what his ... roses are called. It's like a mechanic not ...

Alan See. You're doing it again.

Frank pauses

Frank Yes. Well. It's instinct. That's why I'm a writer.

Alan What're you doing up here if you're a writer? I'n't it a bit hard keeping y'r paper flat?

Frank Obviously I don't write up here. I use this time to plan things out, get the story all in order. Then I go home and write it up.

Alan Have you written owt famous?

Frank Depends what you call famous.

Alan That you can buy in bus stations.

Frank hedges slightly

Frank I have had stuff sold in bus stations. D'you know *The Yorkshireman*?

Alan Who's it by?

Frank The magazine. About Yorkshire.

Alan Oh yeh. The one that's all about moles and dry stone walling.

Frank It's not all about that. It's got the highest circulation of any regional magazine in the north of England.

Pause. Alan sips

Alan 'S mostly people interested in moles read it, though.

Frank Everyone buys it. Doctors buy it, dentists. It's a catalogue of Yorkshire life for anyone. (*Slight pause*) And I've had stuff in there.

Alan A story?

Frank Article.

Alan About what?

Frank (*after a pause*) My childhood in Doncaster.

Alan Oh.

Frank *Paid.*

Alan Mmm.

Frank But I write spy stories mostly. Espionage.

Alan Oh ay. I like them. What, the big thick ones?

Frank Thickness isn't the prime consideration in novel writing.

Alan But they are thick.

Frank But John le Carré doesn't sit down and think "I'm going to write a new novel and I'm not stopping till I get past two and a half inches".

Alan But they are thick. That's why they sell 'em in bus stations. So they take up the whole journey.

Frank John le Carré doesn't spend two years writing a book so it can be a toss up between reading it and having a game of Yah-tzee. Two years of your life goes into it. Two solid inches of thought.

Alan Yes, but sometimes it's a con, because it looks thicker, but the typeset's bigger, so on the page, you get less novel per square inch.

Frank pauses. He looks at Alan over his tea. He didn't expect Alan to know a word like typeset

'Cos sometimes they do it in massive typeset. And nobody notices. Everyone thinks all books come in the same typeset, but if you put some next to each other, you know, some are bigger and some are smaller.

Pause

And some have got little things on the a's and the t's that take up space.

Pause

And some have got proper g's, and some have still got that thing that looks like a duck looking upwards.

Frank frowns. Alan eats some more Twix, this little burst of philosophy over

Frank D'you read a lot of these books then?
Alan Oh yeh. Love 'em.

Frank looks down

Frank I've written three. And some for television. Television spy
   dramas.
Alan Have they been on?

Frank cools

Frank Well, they're, you know. I sent it to the BBC in Leeds, but they
   said they didn't do spy thrillers, they more did local news, and they'd
   send it on to the BBC in London. That's where it is now. It's called *The
   Spy Who Went Out In The Warm.*

Pause

   Like *The Spy Who Came In From The Cold.* It's like an answer to that.
   That's where I got the title from.
Alan Right.
Frank It was going to be *The Spy Who Had A Jumper On,* which was
   one step back, you know. You had to make the connection. But you
   can't have "jumper" in a title. It's just one of those words you can't use.
   Like casserole.
Alan Yeh.
Frank You see, that's where your instinct comes in. You know some
   words won't work in titles. Like *Ice Cold In Alex.* "Ice Cold", it's hard,
   it's direct, it's a good title. But like *Freezing In Alex* — not as good.
   Chilly In Alex, you know. *Bit Nippy in Alex ...*
Alan You couldn't call a novel *Bit Nippy In Alex.*
Frank That's what I'm saying. That's what I'm saying.
Alan No-one'd buy that.
Frank Precisely. That's the instinct you've got to have.
Alan No, you want to call it something like *The Vatican Inheritance.*
   That's a good title. *The Vatican Inheritance.* 'Cos that immediately
   makes you think. You know. It makes you think ... "*What* is the
   Vatican Inheritance?"

Frank cools again

Frank You've read that, have you?

Alan Oh yeh. Great one, that is. Where the bloke is the other bloke's brother and he doesn't know till that other bloke kills him. That's brilliant that is, 'cos you think you've sussed out who the mole is, and it's wrong. And you think someone else is the mole and then that's wrong. And you keep going bam-bam-bam-bam, keep getting it wrong all the way. Then finding out it was the first mole you thought of all along. That's great that is. That's what makes it exciting, you know. When things happen that you didn't expect. (*He stares out a few seconds, relishing the memory of this book*) You didn't write that one, did y'?

Frank Er, no.

Alan Who was it wrote that?

Frank It was, er ... Anthony Belgravia.

Alan Belgravia. That's it. Good, he is. D'you like him?

Pause. Frank stands suddenly and takes his jacket off

Frank Right, let's get the rest up. Mister Forshaw wants these lit up at five thirty to catch the bypass. (*He nods out*)

Alan I haven't finished me tea.

Frank We don't have tea breaks. I told you. We do the job and we get these lit up by five thirty. So come on. Go, go.

Alan (*trudging off*) I'm going.

Frank The r and the s. Get them both and don't knock anything. Lesson two. Don't knock anything. (*He watches Alan*)

Alan disappears behind the glass

Frank thinks a moment

Heads. Bulgovsky looked up at whose hand it was. (*He gasps*) It was Stolichnaya, the old KGB ... (*He pauses, then reconsiders*) No. It was someone more unexpected than that. It was someone incredibly unexpected. A real shock. Complete surprise. Not Stolichnaya. Not

Romanoff. Not Smirnoff. In fact of all the people he could have expected, this was absolutely not one of them, because there, in the cold Leningrad night, completely unexpectedly, stood the one and only ...

Pause

Jimmy Tarbuck.

Pause. He flicks a look to where Alan went off

Unexpected enough? Jimmy Tarbuck, singing "Maybe It's Because I'm A Londoner" accompanied on the car horns by a rack of performing sea lions.

He pauses; then looks out and winces

Bulgovsky waited until the sea lions had finished, then, reaching into his pocket, he pulled out a letter he had received that morning. From Hargreaves and Witton, book publishers.

He produces a letter

("Reading") "Dear Mister Tollit." His breath plumed into frost. "Thank you for sending us your manuscript *A False Hem In The Iron Curtain*. As soon as it arrived we all passed it round the office and had a good laugh, drawing pictures on the front of it and writing 'it's this sad old loser again' on the title page. Then, as our spotty University graduate of a script reader was away, we gave your script to Trixie, a small border terrier, who was passing the front doors. She thought the script was too clichéd and reminiscent of John le Carré and Anthony Belgravia, but she was very complimentary about your typing. Thank you for your interest. If you have any scripts in future, please could you attempt to stick them down the bog at your house, as ours is now jammed with your old ones."

He pauses

There you go, Mister Tarbuck, said Bulgovsky. Was that unexpected?
Not really, said Jimmy, feeding his sea lions.

Alan (*off*) Frank! Eh, Frank!

Frank puts the piece of paper away

Alan appears behind the window

Frank Now what?
Alan Frank!
Frank What?
Alan There's no s.

Frank looks at him

Frank What d'you mean there's no s? Forshaw. F-o-r-s——
Alan I know, but there's no s. I got the r, but there's no s down there anywhere.
Frank Ohhh. (*He sighs*) Bring the h through then.
Alan Yeh, OK. (*He starts to hoick the letters through*) The only thing is, it's not an h. It's an n.

Frank turns

Frank An n?

The two letters are hoisted out. They are indeed an **r** *and an* **n** *. The* **n** *has a kind of attachment on its* R *foot. Frank looks at them both*

(*Suspiciously*) Where have you been getting these from?
Alan The assembled materials despatch bay.
Frank Which pile?
Alan There's only one pile down there.

Frank pauses again

Frank Give me strength. (*He pushes past Alan and goes out through the window*)

Alan Where are you going?

Frank To find out what's going on. Get these bolted to the supports.

Alan On me own?

Frank Yes, on your own. It's your first job. You should be excited. You should be proud. I was proud on my first job.

Frank disappears

*Alan watches him go. He looks dully over to the **F**. He resigns himself to moving it, and tries to lift it. The thing is very awkward. On the top prong, however, he finds the tape he was playing earlier which Frank extracted from the machine. He taps it, then looks behind him. He dips back through the windows and emerges with a double cassette player. The tape goes in and is turned on. The noise is hideous — like a group of Eskimos discovering electric guitars for the first time. But Alan seems to know the words — if you can call them that. He stands on the **n** like a rock star at* Live Aid

Alan (*over the music, pointing at the imaginary crowd*) Leeds, you are the rock and roll centre of the universe.

The music continues. He rethinks

(*Pointing*) Leeds, you are the independent new-wave music centre of the universe. (*He thinks again. Pauses. Pointing*) Leeds, you are a big town off the M62.

*He looks below him at the capital **F** lying on its back. With the music blaring, and miming playing the guitar, he jumps off and, still miming, hoicks it upright. The capital **F** stands there, proudly. Alan salutes it, still energetically "playing" guitar*

Frank appears behind the window, momentarily aghast. He can't believe the racket. He stands a few moments, open mouthed at what Alan is doing

Frank (*finally*) Oi! Oi! *Get that off! Alan!*

Alan turns quickly and swipes off the machine

Have you any idea how far that carries up here?
Alan Sorry.
Frank Appalling bloody racket. Whose it that?
Alan I, er ...
Frank You got it from in there. That's Tracey's. Off that desk. You break her snowstorm, you borrow her stereo ... why don't you go round to her house and throw glue on the carpet?
Alan (*sotto voce*) 'Cos I don't want to.
Frank Why don't you go round and just paint on her windows, eh?

Pause

Mmm?
Alan (*smiling*) Come on.

Pause. Frank frowns like a confused rhino

Come on. There'll be a third one now, won't there? "Why don't you — dot dot dot."

Pause

Frank (*finally, with redoubled force*) *No. There won't.* Get it back in there. And you write the apology this time. These are my colleagues, my friends, Alan, it's not just anybody.

Alan slinks behind the windows

And bring that one out with you. (*He stands, fuming. He wipes his face. Something else is grating him*)

There is a short pause

Alan (*off*) Hey, Frank?
Frank (*murderously*) What?

Alan moves into sight, holding up a letter

Alan We've got two r's.

Frank (*snapping*) I know we've got two r's. I've just found that out, haven't I? I've just brought the bugger up here. I don't need you to tell me that we've got two r's.

Alan looks at it. He deposits the **r**

(*With eyes narrowed*) Someone's cocked it up in planning, haven't they?

Alan Are you sure it's not Forshaw as in "For sure"?

Frank *No.*

Alan Are y' sure?

Frank It's Forshaw. As in new owner of this company. My boss.

Alan D'you want me to go and get the plans?

Frank I don't need a plan to put up the word "Forshaw". I've been doing this twenty-five years. "International Guatemalan Molasses Limited", possibly. But not "Forshaw". On my own building. My own boss's name.

Alan senses the mood

Alan Oh.

Frank How's this going to look, eh? (*He kicks the* **r**)

Alan Not your fault, though.

Frank It's always your fault. Lesson three. When you're doing this, it's not the backroom boys, it's not Brian in design with his bloody red spectacles and his herbal tea who cops it. It's us. Up here. Who look as though we can't spell Forshaw.

Alan But it's not your fault.

Frank Doesn't matter whose fault it is! Doesn't matter if Nicholas Witchell's autocue breaks on the news, people don't think, "That autocue operator wants a good slapping". It's — "Nicholas Witchell, what a git, can't even speak right. I can do that." That's what this'll be. Everyone pointing up, "Can't put letters up in the right order. I could do that". And it's not true. Not anyone could do that. It's a skilled job, this. Not anyone could do it.

Pause. Alan smiles faintly. He nods to the upright **F**

Alan I put this up anyway.

Frank Are you making a point?

Alan No, I'm just saying, I put it up.

Frank And you think it's a doddle.

Alan No ...

Frank Well let me tell you, these are the Rolls Royce of lettering, matey. Three-D self-illuminating. You try putting up vacuum-moulded three-inch thick Toys-'R'-Us on the side of a business unit hanging out of a cradle in a force six. You try putting up IKEA when each letter comes in three sections and each section's the size of Denmark.

Alan I'm not saying it's easy.

Frank This is the easiest one.

Alan All right.

Frank It's the *easiest*.

Alan OK.

Frank pauses

Is there a plan?

Frank rounds on Alan

Frank I am not getting the plan for seven letters. That is exactly what he wants me to do.

Alan Who?

Frank Brian. Brian flaming ... Volvo in design. Brian Mister "Let's give the blue collar workers a different canteen". He comes in with his coloured braces — braces, right, coloured — and he sits behind his draughtsman's board drinking Rose Hip Tea spending three weeks designing "Gateway Fisheries" and he thinks he's Michaelangelo, on some higher plane. I said, "Designing, it's the donkey work, mate. Getting them up there, that's the art." So this is his little challenge, his little (*with a little nibbling away kind of gesture*) getting back. Well I'm not grovelling for a plan. Not so he can say: (*mimicking*) "You want the plan for seven letters, Frank? Losing your touch?" No chance.

Pause. He catches his breath

He wears brass armbands on his sleeves. He's never had his shirt sleeves up in his life.

Pause. The storm abates a little. Alan waits for the dust to go down

Alan Couldn't you use the s from Gateway Fisheries?

Frank (*slowly*) The s on Gateway Fisheries has got a salmon's head coming out of it. Now I think that might possibly give people the wrong impression, don't you? Lesson four. Don't make your letters out of fish unless you're selling haddock. (*He stares at the* n) Anyway. You were right. The whole depot's empty. Every other job must be out. (*He looks at his watch*) You see, if Tracey was back from lunch she'd go and give Brian a rollocking. She's on our side, Tracey is. She's a cracker. (*He sits on the* n)

Alan looks around. He doesn't know what to do

Two r's and an n. Never trust anyone who drives a Volvo. They've all got ulterior motives.

Alan That'd be a good title. "Ulterior Motives".

Frank "Lit up at five thirty to catch rush hour on the bypass, Frank."

Alan You'd have a gun and a playing card and a snake on the cover.

Frank "No problem, Mister Forshaw." It'll be lit up all right. (*Gesturing*) The word Froma.

Alan Or a cocktail glass and some dice and a couple of tickets to Leningrad.

Frank (*turning*) What about Leningrad?

Alan You have them. On the cover of spy books. With a martini and a lizard or something. I put a lizard on my cover.

Frank You haven't had a cover. What cover?

Alan Me band. We did a cassette and I drew the cover. Here. (*He produces the cassette box from his jacket and gives it to Frank*) That's it.

Frank scowls

Frank And what's that lizard supposed to be doing with his tongue hanging out?

Alan Lizard. That's the name of the band. So I drew a lizard.

Frank *You* drew that?

Alan I went to the zoo to get the heads right. (*Nodding towards where the ghetto-blaster was*) That was the tape, just then. We did it in Dixie's front room. Took the curtains down.

Frank looks at it. Then he holds it up

Frank Well, the drawing's good.

Alan Ta. (*He chucks it on his jacket at the back*) D'you think your friend Tracey'd have plans so you didn't have to go to Brian?

Frank *I don't need plans.* I need the right letters. I need an s, an h and a w.

Alan pauses, dully. Then he nods

Alan Well. Depends how you look at it. I mean. If you look at it one way, we've got an s.

Frank looks at him

(*Nodding at where Frank is sitting*) That. Could be. It's got an attachment on it.

Frank looks down at the n

Frank An s?

Alan If y' turn it round.

Frank stands. Alan turns the n *on to its L side*

And that could be what the second r is for. (*He looks underneath the* r) 'S got a bolt. Yeh. See? (*He fits the* r *on to the top of the* n. *It makes a capital* S)

Frank stands in wonder

Frank A capital S. The slippery bastard. He's only gone and done a
   Texan Haulage on me, hasn't he?
Alan A what?
Frank Capital at the beginning and one at the end. Forshaw's. Apostro-
   phe capital s. Try it.

He gestures to Alan to help him move it to the end

   Making the last letter a capital, he thinks that's design. And that's
   worth twenty thousand a year and a Volvo and red braces. Umphhh ...

The **S** *is moved into place at the end. It now reads*:

Fo———S

with an **a** *and an* **r** *kicking about*

   (*Turning, beaming*) Well done, Alan. You see? That's lesson one
   starting to work. You're starting to think ahead. And I tell you, it shows
   you've got an artistic eye as well.
Alan Yeh. I know. (*Moving back towards the windows*) That's what
   they said at college.
Frank And it's important that eye. It means one day, like me, you'll ...
   College?
Alan I'll get the others up.

Alan moves through the back window

Frank Hold on. You — what d'you mean college? You've never been
   to college, you haven't.
Alan (*after a pause*) I know.
Frank (*after a pause*) Right then. (*He frowns*)
Alan It was at the interview.

Alan disappears

Frank Alan! Oi! Come here.

Alan returns

You had an interview?
Alan (*nodding*) Yeh.
Frank To go where?
Alan Art college. Foundation course. You know.
Frank And — and ... did you go?
Alan (*after a pause; it's obvious*) I'm here, aren't I?

Alan goes off

Frank watches him. He is deep in thought. He goes to the cassette box on Alan's jacket. He picks it up, and looks at it

Frank "It's a lizard," thought Bulgovsky. (*After a pause*) And it's a pretty good one as well."
Alan (*off*) Grab this, will y'?

Alan is struggling with a long upright l shape

Frank Is this the h?
Alan Could be. Arghhh.
Frank There you go, you see. Oof.
Alan But the thing is ...

They hoick it on to the ledge

Frank The sky might look black, but there's always one little chink of blue.

It goes up on end. They stand back

That's something at least, eh?
Alan Yeh. There's no round bit, though. (*He gestures to the hump of the h*)

Frank stares at him

Frank Well, that rather kicks it out of the h club then, doesn't it?
Alan S'pose so.

Frank closes his eyes, his world crumbling

Frank And then it all goes black again. (*He drags his face through his hands. He looks at the letters above his fingers*) Something's wrong here, Alan. Something's up. Something is rotten in the state of Batley.

Frank slumps on the **a**. *Alan slumps elsewhere, searching out the remains of his Twix from earlier*

D'you ever get the feeling in life that everything is a test? Everything's put here entirely for your benefit. All the cars on the bypass are all two dimensional, and the fields are supported with wooden struts, and the buildings are all empty apart from the ones you go in? And at a given point this red bell will go off and the sky will get lifted up and this two hundred-mile wide face will be peering down at you, saying: "This one's a pass. Put him back in the pond." (*After a pause*) D'you ever think that?
Alan (*thinking*) No. 'S daft.
Frank (*turning back, a little hurt*) Oh.

Alan pauses and thinks harder

Alan Would never happen, that, would it?
Frank (*piqued*) There are wider things out there we don't understand yet, Alan. There are realms of mystery out there. It's not all "happen — wouldn't happen". (*He sighs*) D'you not wonder about *anything*? Are you happy you know everything you want to about life?

Big pause. Alan thinks very hard

Alan There is one thing. There's one thing I always wonder about. (*Pause*) If you had a train, right. Going at ninety miles an hour from

London to Leeds. (*Pause*) London to anywhere. The Leeds bit doesn't matter. But a train going along in a straight line. And you had one person ready in each joining bit between the carriages, all ready to press their feet down on the pressure things that make the doors open, on a given command. And if you had one person who'd gone to the buffet bar for a Diet Coke, OK? (*Slight pause*) If he shouted "now", and they all pressed down, and the doors all opened and he jumped in the air, why doesn't he end up at the back of the train?

Pause. Frank looks at him

Frank Well, it's (*gesturing loosely*) ... velocity. Isn't it?

Pause

Alan Oh. (*Pause*) Right. Well, I suppose I am pretty happy then.
Frank That's it?
Alan Think so.
Frank I've just answered the only question you had about life? (*He looks at him in disbelief*)
Alan Yeh. (*He looks up, sincerely*) Ta.
Frank There are greater questions to be asked in life, you know.
Alan (*smiling*) You like saying that, don't you?
Frank What?
Alan "In life". You "in life" all the time. Everything's "in life..." something.

Slight pause. Frank frowns slightly

Sounds like there should be a list of them in a book. "In life..." by Frank. Perhaps that should be your next book.
Frank Do I do that?
Alan Yeh.

Pause. Frank evaluates this

Frank You don't miss much, do you? (*Slight pause. He looks down*) Are you going to try again for that college?

Alan (*lost*) Why?

Frank Well, sometimes if they won't have you one time, they'll have you a year after.

Alan Yeh. They prob'ly would've had me last time. If I'd wanted.

Frank You turned it down? You turned down going to college?

Alan It wasn't "college" college. It wasn't Cambridge. It wasn't people walking round with mortar boards on. It was an art foundation course at Batley Tech.

Frank What the hell difference does that make? Why d'you turn it down?

Alan shrugs

   Don't do that.

Alan Do you always get the inquisition when you put up letters?

Frank I'm not inquisitioning. I just want to know ...

Alan Because I didn't want to go. You go if you want to. I didn't want to go. I didn't turn it down. I just didn't go.

Frank But ... that lizard's all right.

Alan Doesn't mean I want to go to college, just 'cos I can draw a good lizard.

Frank What about to get better? Meet people who can get your drawings on the front of books. You don't want that?

Alan pauses

Alan Be all right.

Frank is getting a little lost for words

Frank 'Cos you won't without college. You're up against that lot who come out from Cambridge, you know, Alan. Cambridge churns 'em out, all these rows of shiny-faced graduates who all look like Sebastian Coe. That's who you're up against.

Alan I'm not up against them. I'm up here with you.

Frank Artistically you are.

Alan None of them've seen my lizard. I'm not "up against them".

Frank But you could be. Don't you want to have stuff on the front of books?

Alan thinks

Alan Be all right if it happened.

Frank Oh, and so what, the Happen fairy comes down and throws some Happen dust around and things start to happen?

Alan You like fairies as well, don't you?

Frank What?

Alan You had the Twix fairy before and now we've got the Happen fairy. There's a lot of fairies about.

Frank *They're a metaphor.*

Alan Like the ravens?

Pause

Frank "Illustrated by Alan". You don't want that on the front of the books? You turn down college. You stand about. You do nothing.

Alan (*indignantly*) Yes, I do.

Frank What?

Alan *I enjoy meself.*

Frank Putting up letters on a business unit in Batley?

Alan I thought you were proud of it.

Frank (*after a slight pause*) I am proud of it.

Alan Never sounds like it when you talk about it.

Frank I am proud of it. (*Pause*) But I've got me writing as well, you see. I've got all that. And it's fantastic. When it goes in *The Yorkshireman* and people read it, well, that's the feeling, it's just fantastic.

There is a pause

Like if people read *The Human Experiment*, if it's up there in a long line in bus stations, it's — you couldn't describe it. It makes your back go cold thinking about it. It's like fountains going off inside you. (*He savours it a moment*) Do you not want that?

Pause

Alan What's *The Human Experiment* about?

Pause

Frank (*slightly more subdued*) This bloke who finds out everything on earth is there for his benefit and this bell goes off and there's this two hundred-mile-wide face ...

Alan looks at Frank. Pause. Frank's gaze swings away. He chews his side lip. Alan waits a while. Pause

Alan (*nodding to the distance*) Rush hour's starting.

Frank looks up. The clouds of realization that "The Human Experiment" probably never will be published, which have just appeared on his horizon, are outshadowed by darker ones

Look, d'you reckon your mate Tracey will have a copy ...?
Frank (*patiently*) I don't need the plans. Just bring up what's left.

Alan stands and leaves

(*He stares out*) We'll show Brian-Bloody-Volvo. (*He stands*) *Right.*

He purposefully starts to set the **o** *and* **r** *up into position. Frank stands back. The letters now read:*

$$\textsf{F o r} - \textsf{a} - \textsf{S}$$

With a resurgence of enthusiasm, Frank spaces out where the **h** *is going to be*

Right. OK, Red-Braces. I'll get this word up. Don't you flaming worry about it. We'll see who wins your little tit for tat. (*He pats the* **l**) We'll make an h of you yet. Won't we, Mister Forshaw? "Oh, well done, Frank. I hear the plans were cocked up by Brian and you still got the word up for five thirty."

Alan (*off*) Frank?
Frank "What would I do without you?" Go, go! I'm ready.
Alan (*off*) Frank?
Frank I'm ready, bring them out. Go, go!

Alan emerges

Alan There's only an e.
Frank What?
Alan (*holding it up*) That's all there is left.
Frank There were stacks of letters at the back. I saw them.
Alan Those were all broken.

Frank laughs

Frank (*stepping out the spaces*) They weren't broken ones!
Alan They were.
Frank No, they look broken, but they're called Independent Angle
  Assembly Modules. You see, w, it's a tricky letter ——
Alan Frank! They were broken! They were in bits. The ends were
  splintered and half of them were green.

Pause

Frank Green?
Alan They were rubbish. This is it. (*He holds the* **e** *up*) This is all that's
  left. This is the end.
Frank (*after a pause*) No w?
Alan Look, why don't you see if Tracey's got a copy of the plan.

Frank fumes silently

Frank (*grimly*) We'll wait.
Alan The office must have a copy of ——
Frank We'll wait till she gets back. I'm not giving in to him.
Alan But Frank ——
Frank *I'm not giving in.*

Alan Frank ——

Frank He's scared, you see. He knows when this company expands it's going to be dog eat dog, and he's trying to prove himself . Well, we don't play up to him. We wait till Tracey gets back off lunch.

Pause

Alan Frank.
Frank (*after a pause*) What.
Alan It's five fifteen. She's not going to be at lunch, is she?

Frank looks at his watch

I don't think she's coming back.

Frank is faced with a brick wall. This is true. No way out. He grits his teeth. And he nods

Frank Right. All right. OK. If that's the way it is, that's the way it bloody is. (*He stands*)
Alan What are you doing?
Frank (*reaching for his jacket*) I'm going to have him. I'm going down to design and I'm going to have him. If he wants me to play into his hands he'll find I'm a bit of a prickly customer, is old Frank.
Alan Hold on.
Frank Oh yes. Lesson four.
Alan Six.
Frank (*thinking a second*) *Four.* (*He goes to Alan and starts coming all godfatherly again*) You, Alan. Me. We're what's important in this palaver. We're the ones out there doing it. It's *us* that's important. And you have to remember that. 'Cos the Brians, they all know that, but they don't like it. And they try and spread their feathers, pull rank. So we stay professional, we keep our personal feelings out of the way. But we don't take mess from anyone.

Pause

(*Louder*) Especially not from twenty-eight year olds who went to Cambridge and drink herbal tea and take three weeks to design the word Gateway Fisheries.

Frank stomps off and out

Alan Frank! Frank!

But Frank has gone. Alan turns. He looks at the letters, and winces into the evening breeze. He's a bit worried

(*Quieter*) Frank.

He looks round, guiltily, and makes up his mind. He slips through the window into the office. He searches around fruitlessly a while, but then clocks the large filing cabinet. Flicking a look over his shoulder he stands on a chair and pulls open the top drawer. He scrabbles through some files and finally pulls one out. He opens it. He unfolds a large piece of paper

Oh 'eck.

Now really worried, he gets off the chair and comes back on to the ledge. He looks at the paper. Then at the letters. He moves the l *L a bit. He looks at the plan again. He moves the* **a** *to stand* R *of the* l *. The letters now read:*

For — alS

Then Alan looks at the plan, and up at the giant capital **S** *. He shuffles it like a menhir round* R *of the* **a**. *The letters now read:*

For Sal

He stands back. The expression worsens

Oh 'eck.

He slowly, fatefully, looks at the remaining e propped against the wall

   *At that second, like a spectre, Frank appears in the window. But his
   whole attitude has changed. His is the expression of fresh raw grief
   which hasn't got past the stunned stage*

   (Weakly, quietly) All right, Frank?

*Alan looks at him through the glass. Then he chews his lip. The wind
blows traffic noise across the ledge. Frank walks out. He seems to know
already, he isn't surprised. He looks at the letters. And slowly he nods*

   I ... er ... found the plans.

Frank looks back at the opened filing cabinet

   I was going to put it back.

Frank looks at the letters again. He bites his lip

Frank Well. Better get it finished.

He starts to heave the e up to the end. It now reads, quite clearly:

For Sale

Alan looks down

Alan Did Brian tell you?

Frank stares out over the e. He breathes in heavily

   I suppose you were attached to this place, weren't y'? Must be tough
   moving somewhere else after twenty-five years.

Slight pause

He'll just be expanding, yeh? Bigger premises, like you said. There's a lot of companies needing letters now, with these new business parks.

Frank pauses. Then he nods, slowly

Still. 'S not the best way to hear it, off Brian.

Pause

Frank Brian wasn't there. (*He holds out a piece of paper*)
Alan Where was this?
Frank Design noticeboard.

Alan takes it

Alan (*reading*) "Would all employees of Forshaw Lettering involved in the company relocation to Otley please ensure they attend the briefing afternoon. Friday, September fourteenth." (*He looks back at the empty office*)
Frank Doesn't look like the relocation fairy stopped at my house.

There is an end-of-the-world kind of pause

(*Suddenly he breathes in. Rallying*) Well, there we go. Nearly half-five. Let's get these cabled up. (*He resumes*)

Alan stands dumbfounded

Alan (*gesturing to the notice*) Aren't you going to do anything?

Frank seizes the coil of cable out of his toolbag

But — but you're putting yourself out of a job, doing that, Frank. Doing your job is putting yourself out of one. It's like a dry-stone waller smashing himself over the head with a rock.
Frank Grab this cable, will you?
Alan No. I won't. I'm not.

Frank (*pointing at the plans*) That's the construction brief. F-o-r-S-a-l-e. Doesn't matter if it's any old company or your own company, you ... (*He feeds the cable out*)

Alan Ah come on, don't start that old trooper rubbish.

Frank Alan, in life ——

Alan Don't. Don't "in life" me. I'm fed up of being "in life-d". Why don't you try "in life-ing" yourself. Lesson eight.

Frank Three.

Alan *Seven.*

Frank *He's selling up, Alan.* Mister Forshaw is relocating. "As long as there's a Forshaw lettering plant here, there'll be a job for you, Frank." (*Gesturing to the* **For Sale** *letters*) OK? Mm? (*He actually goes and stands in the gap between the words*) Clever, eh? Clever way with words. (*He moves through, and edges along the sheer ledge in front of the word* **For**)

Alan stands, worried. He doesn't know what Frank is intending to do

You see ... I thought it all through. Between the vending machine and here. (*Slight pause*) Where the vending machine was. (*He looks out at the horizon, resting on the* **o**)

Alan (*quietly*) You're not going to jump off, are you? (*Pause*) It's just I wouldn't have anyone to fill in me assessment form.

Frank (*staring out at the horizon*) What are you doing here, Alan?

Alan Calling the police if you don't come away from there.

Frank You can draw.

Alan You can write. And that's a ledge, and that's sixty feet down and there's very little difference.

Frank Oh no, no. You see, that's the thing. (*He sits on the* **o**) I want to write. But I have this problem, you see, Alan. I have this problem. And, you see, the problem is — I'm crap.

Alan doesn't know what to say to this

I didn't ask for it. I didn't *ask* to want to write. But when God sat up there and gave me this terrible burning ... (*he searches for words*) ... *burn* to see my name up in bus stations — and he did, Alan, Christ, he did — when he gave me that, he said, "Here you go, Frank. And just to make it a little more interesting, I'll give you the ambition, but absolutely no talent. Absolutely bugger all."

Pause

And then he sat back and he laughed himself stupid.
Alan You're all right.

Frank leans back on the word **For**

Frank "Two dimensional characterization. Rip off of other writers. Clichéd phrases." It's official. Ask the publishers.
Alan You've had stuff published.
Frank In *The Yorkshireman*. Yes. I have. And you know what it was about?
Alan Your childhood.
Frank No. Moles. You were right first time. I lied.
Alan Look, I didn't mean — I mean, I like moles ...
Frank When I write about any other kind of moles, spy moles, what happens is Bulgovsky, OK, he walks over this bridge in Leningrad, right, through the cold Leningrad night, and what happens is he meets George Smiley. And Smiley points and he says, "Hold on, Bulgovsky. You're just a poor version of me, aren't you?" And Bulgovsky hasn't got anything to say to that. He just sort of fades away.
Alan Ah come on, stop all this. It takes ages to get it right. Tons of them start late. John le Carré, Len ... I bet Anthony Belgravia didn't start till he was ——
Frank Eighteen. (*Pause*) In Leeds. Twenty-four, Fontainebleu Road, Meanwood, Leeds.

Pause

Great garden at the back for playing football. Beech tree and a pear. Lives in Capri now. Married to an actress.
Alan You knew Anthony Belgravia?
Frank Tony Bell. (*Pause*) I sent him copies of my novels in the

beginning. But he never wrote back. Last Christmas I sent him a copy of *The Yorkshireman* to show him I'd had something published. (*He half laughs*) He's having Sean Connery in a film of his book, and I sent him a copy of *The Yorkshireman* about mole repellants.

Alan Did he read it?

Frank (*shrugging*) He didn't mention it when he was on *Wogan*.

Alan He's been back then?

Frank Oh yes. He flew in once from America to do a book signing at Dillons in Leeds.

Pause

You see, I know about that, Alan. I was the one who put up the letters saying he was coming. (*He frames them in the sky*) "Anthony Belgravia. In this store today." Nice, they were. Three-D. Self-illuminating. Big stars get big letters. (*He thinks*) Anthony Belgravia. And I was up that ladder. (*He looks out*) And I felt so far away from it all, Alan. It was all so far away. All that ... land somewhere where people get their names printed on books, where they live in Capri with actresses, and fly in from America. I was just so ... far away. With my repeating phrases. And my Batley-Leningrad.

Pause

You see, he'll've been to Leningrad. He'll actually have been there. I get the names off vodka bottles.

Alan Well, if it's getting to you, forget it. Do something else.

Frank (*smiling*) You really don't care if no-one sees your lizard, do you?

Alan No. I don't, that much.

Frank If you never illustrate a book, if it's never up in that bus station.

Alan No. 'Cos I'm having a good time. I'm having a good time with the rest of it, aren't I?

Frank You really wouldn't care.

Alan No.

Frank just stares out

No, not that much.

Pause

Frank You know, Alan? I wish I was you.

Alan is incredulous. He shakes his head

Alan Impossible.
Frank (*nodding*) Mm-mm.
Alan No-one can wish they were like me. It's impossible.
Frank I wish I didn't care when I see books in bus stations. I wish I could just buy one and not think "*I* want to be there, I want to see *The Spy Who Went Out In The Warm* up there. But I won't. It's rubbish. I know it is. But that doesn't stop anything. That doesn't put it out. And trying to take pride in all this ... (*He kicks the letters. Shaking his head*) Doesn't work. 'Cos you try to for a bit, then suddenly — brinnng! Somewhere in the sky this huge red bell goes off, and the lid comes off and there's Bulgovsky's face. Two hundred miles wide. Shouting, "You're not really proud of it, Frank. Not putting up plastic letters of other people's names." And he picks me off that bridge in Leningrad. And he puts a tag round my leg saying "fail". And he chucks me into the river.

Pause

Alan What d'you want, Frank? Really?
Frank In life?
Alan In life.
Frank I'd like to be immortal. Just for a bit. Just ... like old Lord Preston with his folly up there. You can still see him. All the cars on the bypass, they all still see him every night. He's still up there. He had the right idea. (*He pauses*) I bet he wanted to write spy novels, too.

Alan looks out at the folly. Suddenly something galvanizes in his mind

Alan (*quietly*) Frank? Will you do something for me?

Pause

Will you let me finish it off?

Frank looks at him

Frank What?
Alan Cable it up. Will you go and stand out there. Other side of the
bypass. Where everyone else will be looking at it. Tell me what it looks
like?

Pause

It's me first job.

*Frank nearly smiles. He looks out again. Then finally he nods, slowly,
like a warrior accepting inevitable defeat*

Frank (*quietly*) OK. (*He stands and surveys the skyline*)
Alan I want to be proud of it.

*Frank edges off the ledge. He picks up his jacket and tool bag and silently
moves towards the window. Then a thought gets through to him. He stops
and hands his tool bag to Alan*

(*Quietly*) Lesson one.

And with that, Frank walks through the window and off

*Alan watches him go. He looks at his watch. Then with a burst of energy,
he grabs and spools out the cable, plugging in the* **F** *and the* **r** *. He stands
back, a sense of feverish determination is spreading across his face. He
drags back the* **a** *, and swaps it with the* **S** *. The letters now read:*

ForaSle

(*Grittedly*) I want to be proud of it.

He pushes the **e** *completely out of the way, and disengages the capital* **S** *to form a sideways* **n** *and an* **r** *. He tips the sideways* **n** *upright again, and whips the cable along to plug in the* **a, n,** *and* **l** *. At the end of the row near the junction box* UL *he drops the second* **r** *. Then he plugs the end of the cable into the junction box. The letters now read:*

Foranlr

He stands back, panting. He smiles. Then he summons up all he's got left

(*Shouting*) It's Friday. It's half-past five. And are you ready, Batley?

With a dramatic flourish, he pushes the second **r** *back at an angle against the* **l** *, throws the switch, snatches up his coat and leaves*

Black-out. The neon lights come up. The **l** *and* **r** *now form a* **k** *. And Alan has not connected up the* **o** *. So the neon sign over the Batley skyline tonight reads:*

F rank

Music bursts in

CURTAIN

FURNITURE AND PROPERTY LIST

On stage: *In office*
        Large sliding window closed
        Filing cabinet. *In it*: file containing large plan
        Dead pot plant
        Chair

        On ledge
        Wall-mounted electricity junction box UL

Off stage: Red capital letter F* (**Frank** and **Alan**)
        Red lower case a* (**Frank** and **Alan**)
        Two polystyrene cups, plastic-wrapped two-pack of di-
            gestive biscuits, red lower case o* (**Alan**)
        Red lower case r and n (with attachment on its r foot)*
            (**Alan**)
        Ghetto blaster (**Alan**)
        Red lower case r* (**Alan**)
        Red lower case l* (**Alan**)
        Red lower case e* (**Alan**)
        Memo sheet (**Frank**)

Personal: **Frank**: wrist-watch, huge ring of keys, paper and pen,
            coins, letter, leather toolkit containing coil of cable and
            heavy-looking socket on one end
        Alan: Walkman stereo with cassette tape, 5 Twix bars,
            wrist-watch, cassette box with an inlay card bearing a
            drawing of a lizard

*The upper case letter F and the upright l should be approximately six
feet high and the lower case letters a, o, r, n, and e should be approximately three-feet high. For further information please see the author's
note on page vi.

LIGHTING PLOT

Property fittings required: nil

Exterior. The same scene throughout

To open: General autumn afternoon effect, gradually darkening

Cue 1   **Alan** snatches up his coat and leaves   (Page 43)
             Black-out. Then bring up u.v. effect on letters

EFFECTS PLOT

Cue 1	Before the Lights come up *Music; distant hum of traffic noise*	(Page 1)
Cue 2	As the Lights come up *Fade music; punctuate pauses with distant hum of traffic noise throughout play*	(Page 1)
Cue 3	**Frank**: "One one-way ticket to Leningrad." *Loud glass-smash*	(Page 5)
Cue 4	**Frank**: "...at finishing school in Switzerland." *Huge glass-smash*	(Page 10)
Cue 5	**Alan** switches on the ghetto blaster *Loud rock music*	(Page 20)
Cue 6	**Alan** turns quickly and swipes off the machine *Cut rock music*	(Page 21)
Cue 7	Neon lights come up *Burst of music*	(Page 43)

Printed by The Kingfisher Press, London NW10 7AS